Jessie J
Annual 2013

Posy Edwards

Meet Jessie J...

She's a pop star, a TV star, and a songwriter who has overcome childhood illness to become one of the top talents in music. With her role as a TV judge, she's helped other wannabe singers too, and has become an even bigger star along the way.

With number one hits the world over, it looks like the girl from Essex – who has written songs for Alicia Keys and counts Justin Timberlake as one of her biggest fans – is conquering the world!

Jessie J fact file

FULL NAME: Jessica Ellen Cornish

DATE OF BIRTH: 27th March 1988

BORN AND RAISED: Chadwell Heath, Essex

HEIGHT: 5ft 9in

EDUCATION: Mayfield High School, Redbridge and The BRIT School, Croydon

FAMILY: Dad is social worker, Stephen, Mum is nursery school teacher, Rose, and two sisters, Hannah and Rachel

FAVOURITE COLOURS: Red and pink

FAVOURITE FOOD: West Indian and Japanese food, and Sunday roasts!

FAVOURITE SINGER: Rihanna

FAVOURITE SONG: 'You're The One For Me' by D Train

FIRST CONCERT SHE WENT TO: The boyband Five at Wembley

CELEBRITY CRUSH: Simon Cowell

FAVOURITE MEMBER OF ONE DIRECTION: Niall. 'He's sweet, he's got blonde hair and he got very excited when he won a BRIT award and it was really cute'

FIRST BAND: The Three Cornish Pasties, formed with her two sisters! (Hannah on piano, Rachel on trombone and Jessie on vocals)

THE SUPERPOWER SHE WOULD LIKE TO HAVE: To be able to fly or be invisible

ALTERNATIVE CAREER: A therapist or something to do with fashion

On 27th March, 1988, Jessica Ellen Cornish was born in the London suburb of Chadwell Heath. The daughter of Rose and Stephen, she grew up in Essex with two older sisters, Hannah and Rachel, and went to the local Mayfield school where both her sisters had been head girls.

From an early age, Jessie knew she wasn't going to be academic like her siblings, and her parents knew, too – her first words as a baby were 'jam hot', the lyrics to the 1990 hit 'Dub Be Good To Me'.

In fact, she remembers she was 'a little show-off' as a toddler, telling jokes to anyone who would listen, and singing whenever she could. 'At school, they were like "oh, you're a Cornish girl" and they kind of expected me to be the same as my sisters. Give me something to draw or an outfit to pick for someone, or hair, make-up, acting, write a song, I'm fine with it, but anything to do with sums – it was never my thing.'

A Star is Born

'I think I ooze British. I'm very sarcastic and I like to take the mickey out of myself. And I definitely do that very British thing of taking things with a pinch of salt.'

Her parents encouraged her to perform, but her first few attempts at appearing live were less than successful: when she auditioned for a stage production of *Annie* at the age of 10, she didn't get the part because she was 'too loud' and the same thing happened when she tried out for her school choir. 'I was in it for a day and some of the adults were moaning that their kids were upset that I was too good,' Jessie remembers. 'I was 11. Can you imagine? I was heartbroken.'

Her school friend Kirstie Kober, whose mum Dawn taught Jessie ballet, remembers that singing was Jessie's favourite activity, no matter where she was. 'My mum taught us ballet and in the middle of the class Jessica would be singing and making up lyrics to go along with the classical music we were doing our ballet exercises to,' Kirstie remembers. 'Mum would say: "Jessica, this is a ballet class, not a singing lesson, please get on with your plié."'

'I wasn't always someone who was talented. It was more that I was loud and loved a challenge.'

Finding her career

Jessie wouldn't be sad for long. When she wasn't listening to her favourite soul and funk music (the songs of Aretha Franklin, Michael Jackson and Prince often blared from her bedroom) or pretending to be in a girl band with her sisters (called The Three Cornish Pasties!), she went to auditions, and in 1999 she won a role in the West End musical *Whistle Down The Wind*, written by famous producer Andrew Lloyd Webber and based on a 1961 movie of the same name.

Whistle Down The Wind is probably best known for the song 'No Matter What', recorded by Boyzone. It tells the story of three children – Swallow, Poor Baby and Brat – in rural Louisiana, who find a man hiding in their barn. When Swallow startles him, he cries out 'Jesus Christ' and then passes out, leaving her to think that he really is the son of God, whereas in reality he's an escaped killer and the grown-ups of the town are out looking for him.

On the stage and off it!

Jessie was one of the children chosen to play the role of Swallow's younger sister, Brat (*Hollyoaks* star Hannah Tointon also played the same role), and she played the part for two years, squeezing in performances between her school lessons. 'I think it was that that made me grow up really fast because I was going through school to do a show every night. It made me realise that I could do what I love and be paid for it.'

One particular performance was quite memorable: she fell off stage! 'I was singing 'When Children Rule the World' and as I hopped to go off stage, my foot went into the orchestra pit and I did a back flip onto the conductor,' she laughs. 'I was splattered all over the orchestra, sheets of music everywhere.' After that, Andrew Lloyd Webber made sure he met her to check she was okay. 'I think he was worried I was going to sue him,' she jokes.

Just Jessie 'I want to be a positive role model for young people. I always say that I am half-artist, half-therapist.'

Health Problems

Jessie's road to fame from child stage singer to pop star wasn't always a smooth one – the first bump came one day when she was out with her father and sister. 'I remember me and my dad and my sister were in Epping Forest and my dad said, "Let's race to the car." And I just collapsed. They were like, "Stop messing around!" But I couldn't breathe and I just went white and got rushed to hospital.'

It turned out Jessie had a heart defect, similar to her dad Stephen's. 'I remember my mum and dad saying: "You're just like Daddy, you've got a special heart." Even now, every time I get sick my dad feels so guilty, like it's his fault.' The heart problem is called Wolff-Parkinson-White syndrome, and the medicine Jessie had to take meant that she couldn't do sport at school and her skin turned a shade of green. 'I used to get called Alien', she remembers. 'I always had to take it slow otherwise I'd end up in hospital.'

Just Jessie

'I want to be at the top. I want to be a credible artist, not just someone here today and gone tomorrow. You're not going to get rid of me.'

'I want people to know that I sit with no make-up on in my pyjamas in my bedroom hanging out. I'm normal. I don't always look like this.'

First steps to fame – The BRIT School

Once she had her illness under control, Jessie began regular weekend dance lessons, and when she was 16, she joined the BRIT school, learning musical theatre. It was a good place to study. The London School for Performing Arts & Technology in Croydon – better known as the BRIT School – was set up in 1991 and provides training in the performing arts, media, art and design by a group led by Mark Featherstone-Witty, who had been inspired by the movie *Fame* (which is set in the real life La Guardia Arts school in New York).

It boasts some famous former students, too, including singers Amy Winehouse, Imogen Heap, Kate Nash, Katy B, Leona Lewis and Katie Melua, Inbetweeners actors Blake Harrison and Emily Head, and the bands The Kooks and The Feeling. One of her classmates was Adele, whom Jessie remembers well. 'She was in music and I was in musical theatre [classes]. We used to jam at lunchtime and someone would play guitar and we both would just sing. At the time we both didn't know we'd have albums out at the same time. And she's killing it. I'm so proud of her. [At school] she was very loud and everyone knew her. She was the girl everyone loved and she was always up for a laugh. You could hear her from a mile down the corridor!'

A BRIT school friend of Jessie's, Kerry Louise Barnaby, remembers that Jessie didn't yet have her trademark black bobbed hair or catsuits when she was at the school. 'She didn't have a fringe; her hair was just long and straight. She didn't wear much make-up. She'd wear skinny jeans, a plain baggy t-shirt and Converse trainers. That was it, that was Jess.'

Going Solo

Soul Deep

While Jessie was at the BRIT School, she formed a girl group with two friends called Soul Deep, and in 2005 the girls were talent-spotted by music manager Raymond Stevenson. He encouraged Jessie to listen to different types of music, like Kanye West and Missy Elliott, and find her own sound.

Just as things were looking up however, tragedy struck. A few months before she was due to graduate, Jessie suffered a minor stroke and had to drop out. 'I was tired and stressed and that combined with my heart...' she says. 'I had four jobs, I was in a girl group – I blame it on being in a girl group! They're not easy!'

The stroke made her realise it was time to get a move on if she wanted to launch her singing career. 'You know when people go, "You're 18 and you've got all the time in the world?" I was like: "Well, no. I've just had a stroke and I don't think I do."' Soul Deep went their separate ways soon after, but it was when Jessie decided to strike out on her own that things began to happen...

Big Break

When she was 17, everything started to change for Jessie. To pay for singing lessons, she worked as a hair model for salon Vidal Sassoon ('I looked like an idiot but it paid for my singing lessons, I had a Mohawk, a mullet, all sorts!') and one of the haircuts they gave her was similar to the fringed bob she often has now.

It wasn't just her look that was changing. In 2005, she signed to Gut Records, a label that also had artists including Jessie's future fellow *The Voice* judge Tom Jones on its books. Gut put her on tour with well-known stars like Sugababes, Cyndi Lauper and Chris Brown and Jessie got ready to record an album, but Gut closed down before it could be released. Undeterred, she headed for Los Angeles, found an agent, and began to perform at small music venues. And when she wasn't singing, Jessie was writing new songs – songs that famous artists couldn't wait to snap up.

I write the songs

While she continued to write songs for herself, Jessie also penned songs for Alicia Keys ('L.O.V.E') and Chris Brown ('I Need This'). But it was a song she wrote for herself that was then recorded by someone else that would give Jessie her first number one hit.

She was working with Britney Spears' producer, Dr Luke, and together they wrote a song called 'Party In The USA'. 'I remember the [record] label saying, "This is a hit, but it's not edgy enough for you." So we pitched it to Miley Cyrus, and within three weeks she recorded it and it went to number one. So I still, to this day, don't know how amazing that is.'

Released in the US in the summer of 2009, it became Hannah Montana star Miley's biggest hit to date, and the sixth biggest selling single of the year in the US. It was also a change of direction for the American singer with a squeaky clean image. 'There are so many friends of mine that would say, "I would never, ever, ever listen to Miley Cyrus, like, as Hannah Montana" and it kind of brought her over to another style,' remarks Jessie.

Just Jessie 'As a songwriter, I'm still taking baby steps. You have to write 10 songs to get one good one.'

Five years and 600 songs

Jessie had started working on her debut album back in 2006 when she was signed to Gut Records, but it wasn't until 19th January 2011 that it was finally finished and ready for release. Over those five years, she changed record labels, wrote songs for other artists and wrote a whopping 600 songs for herself!

Just Jessie

'At the moment, I'm single and I'm happy and learning about myself. Music is the love of my life right now.'

It was decided that the album would be called *Who You Are* after one of its songs, and the first track to be released would be 'Do It Like A Dude'. Released as a download in November 2010, the song was actually meant for someone else! 'I wrote it with Rihanna in mind because [her song] 'Rude Boy' was out at the time and that's kinda what inspired me to write the song. At first I never really saw myself doing something like it, but I knew I could. I sent it to my label and I was like, "I'm just sending you this before I send it to Rihanna's camp to see if you guys like it." And they were like, "This is your first single. It's amazing."'

Jessie J arrives

Just Jessie

'I think the best way to have confidence is not to allow everyone else's insecurities to be your own.'

Like a Dude

Jessie's inspiration for the song came when she was working in a recording studio and two producers named Parker and James came in. 'One of them wears his trousers ridiculously low,' Jessie remembers. 'So I just started free styling like a dude, and it was fun. I wanted to write a song that was tongue-in-cheek and a parody of a stereotypical male. But also, I wanted the song to be empowering for girls, but not kind of an "I hate men" song – because I don't, and I don't say that in the song. It's about feeling hardcore.'

The song went straight in at number 25 on the UK Singles Chart on 28th November 2010, and by 16th January 2011 it had reached number 2, only held off the number one spot by Bruno Mars' mega-selling 'Grenade'. Jessie J had arrived...

Who You Are

Before her album was released, it was time to bring out a second single, and the song chosen was 'Price Tag'. Written by Jessie with Dr Luke, Claude Kelly and rapper B.o.B (who also raps on the song), it would be the track that turned Jessie into a music superstar.

With an eye-catching video that became a huge hit on YouTube and a memorable reggae bounce, the song went straight to number one in the UK on 6th February 2011. It also went to number one in Belgium, France, Ireland and New Zealand, and made the top ten in Australia, Canada, Germany, Italy, the Netherlands, Norway and Switzerland. There was no time to enjoy the success, however, as Jessie's album *Who You Are* came out just three weeks later!

Who You Are: The Songs

Price Tag

Nobody's Perfect

Abracadabra

Big White Room

Casualty Of Love

Rainbow

Who's Laughing Now

Do it Like A Dude

Mamma Knows Best

L.O.V.E

Stand Up

I Need This

Who You Are

Platinum Edition bonus tracks: Domino, My Shadow, LaserLight

The album was originally supposed to be released on 28th March 2011, but Jessie's website announced the new, earlier release date: 'Newsflash! Due to phenomenal demand, we are going to let you have Jessie J's debut album a month early! Jessie said, 'I'm in a whirlwind right now, I'm loving every minute of it. Can't wait for the world to hear the album that I've been working on for the last six years. Bring it on!'

Just Jessie 'I'm like a little girl with a dream.'

Under Pressure

And the Winner is...

2011 had only just begun and Jessie J already had two hit singles and a new album to her name – not bad for a 22-year-old! She was winning awards, too – at the end of 2010 she was named the winner of the BBC's Sound Of 2011 award, and on 15th February 2011, Jessie won the Critics' Choice award at the BRITs, an award for upcoming talent that had previously been won by Adele, Florence And The Machine and Ellie Goulding, who presented the award with producer Mark Ronson to Jessie in front of a TV audience of millions.

'There's not many times in my life that I'm speechless, as some of you probably know,' Jessie said as she accepted the award, 'but I didn't plan anything to say, apart from this – I remember sitting over there [she points to the audience] trying to get the attention of anyone and now I'm sitting here and collecting an award. It's amazing. For anyone who has been with me on my journey, from six years ago when I first got signed, or last week if you downloaded my song or watched me sing in my pyjamas on YouTube, I just want to say from the bottom of my heart, thank you for making my dreams come true.'

Stage Jitters

With a new hit album to promote, it was time for Jessie to hit the stage. While she already had a reputation for being one of the best artists to see live from the small gigs she had performed before she was well known, it wasn't always plain sailing. In early February 2011, Jessie performed at a special gig called 'Black Out', and she suffered a panic attack on stage. 'The night was called Black Out and I had to perform in the dark. I asked them to turn on the lights and they didn't. I was on stage in the pitch black and, because I couldn't see anything, I started to panic. It was awful.' No one in the audience was aware anything was wrong, as Jessie carried on despite the panic attack.

Just Jessie

'If I'm a singer I have to be good at singing. Singing live for me is my time to go: "this is what I am good at."

Falling down

This wasn't her only stage mishap in 2011. In June, she was in rehearsals for the Capital Radio Summertime Ball that was to take place at Wembley Stadium in London, and featured artists like Cee Lo Green, JLS, The Wanted and Jennifer Lopez. Unfortunately, while practising her performance the day before the mega-gig, Jessie fell from a platform and tore tendons in her foot. Not wanting to let her fans down, Jessie was a true trooper and performed at the ball… sitting on a golden throne, with her foot heavily bandaged and covered in a white sock! She stood to sing 'Do It Like A Dude', then gave in and sat on the throne for the rest of her performance.

'I fell off the stage and mashed up my foot – I ruptured all the tendons in it,' she told the crowd of 75,000 at the stadium. 'I was told to stay at home. But I said: "Are you crazy? I'm not letting my fans down." I did ask for a crystal sock to cover the bandage but this is all they had.' Clearly in pain, she added: 'Sometimes it's best to follow the doctor's orders. Why couldn't I be an artist who just wears trainers?!'

Just Jessie

'My mum and dad have both devoted their lives to saving other people's lives and I want to do the same – I want my music to save people's lives. And I won't stop.'

Powering on

Jessie had been scheduled to appear at other gigs throughout the summer, but while some artists would have stayed at home to allow their foot to heal, she carried on, appearing at the Glastonbury Festival, once again singing from the throne after walking onto the stage on crutches. Making sure she was festival chic, she even had an assistant come on stage and help her put a high-heeled black PVC boot on her good foot!

It turned out that Jessie had been misdiagnosed – she hadn't pulled the tendons in her foot, she'd actually broken it and would have to spend six weeks on crutches with her foot in plaster. Her doctors told her enough was enough, and Jessie was forced to cancel appearances at T In The Park, Lovebox and the iTunes Festival over the summer. 'Sorry doesn't feel enough to say,' she told her fans, 'I am devastated for my fans that I know have been waiting to see me and working hard for tickets. I was so excited about the summer and I'm as upset as you all are. But unfortunately these things happen.' The injury meant Jessie was going to have to have surgery on her foot, and she told fans she was 'super-scared'. She tweeted: 'Keep making nervous jokes with the doctor and he keeps looking at me blankly. Which is making me laugh even more. It's getting serious. I just took my nose stud out.' She kept fans – whom she calls her 'heartbeats' – up to date with news, however, and tweeted after the surgery: 'Can't keep tweeting. Still very dizzy and being sick. But I'm ok, I got through it.'

Back on track

The surgery didn't keep Jessie away for long, and by August she was performing again, still with one leg strapped up (in a very cool, blinged-up cast) and often singing from a chair. She performed at the V Festival like this, complete with purple hair, and also at the MTV Video Music Awards in Los Angeles, where she was the 'house artist', performing her hits to the celebrity crowd and mixing them with cool covers of Cyndi Lauper's 'Girls Just Want To Have Fun', Katy Perry's 'Firework', Cee Lo Green's 'Forget You' and TLC's classic 'No Scrubs'.

Despite her broken foot, Jessie didn't have time to stop. A new track from the album, 'Who's Laughing Now', was released on 10th August, and, with its video featuring a young Jessie look-alike standing up to kids who had teased her, it soon became known as an anthem against bullying. 'This song makes me laugh,' Jessie said. 'I have had so many supporters but also many non-believers and this track is my "ha-ha!" to them. As I say: "let the haters hate, they're like way too late."'

Jessie herself appears as a dinner lady, school cleaner and a teacher in the video. 'Music is about making a change but also being able to laugh at yourself. I think this song tells a story a lot of people have been through and I hope it will raise awareness to the serious issue of bullying.'

Quick Quiz

How well do you know Jessie? Try our quick quiz and find out...

1) Which well known singer did Jessie go to school with? Was it:

a) Tinie Tempah

b) Adele

c) Ellie Goulding

d) Katy Perry

2) Jessie sang a duet called 'Up' with a famous male singer. Was it:

a) Eminem

b) Tom Jones

c) Bruno Mars

d) James Morrison

3) What's Jessie's favourite food?

a) Spaghetti bolognese

b) Pizza

c) Fish and chips

d) Extra hot and spicy curry

4) Which one of these artists hasn't recorded a song written by Jessie?

a) Chris Brown

b) Christina Aguilera

c) Alicia Keys

d) Britney Spears

5) Jessie J helped one of the judges choose their final acts on the X Factor in 2011. But which judge did she work with?

a) Simon Cowell

b) Cheryl Cole

c) Louis Walsh

d) Tulisa Contostavlos

6) During The Voice's blind auditions, one of the performers was a male singer who used to be in a boyband Jessie loved when she was younger. She didn't recognise him, though! Who was it?

a) Gary Barlow from Take That

b) Duncan James from Blue

c) Sean Conlon from Five

d) Matt Willis from Busted

7) The Voice judges sang together on stage but what song did they sing?

a) 'It's Not Unusual'

b) 'I Gotta Feeling'

c) 'Price Tag'

d) 'Where Is The Love?'

8) Which animal would Jessie most like to be?

a) Cat

b) Micro-pig

c) Dog

d) Fluffy rabbit

9) What is Jessie's favourite shopping street in London?

a) Carnaby Street

b) Oxford Street

c) Knightsbridge, because Harrods is there

d) The Westfield shopping centre

10) In 2011, Jessie surprised fans by singing along to a boombox and busking for the passengers and passers-by at a station. Where was she?

a) Leicester Square tube station in London

b) The Gare Du Nord in Paris

c) Manchester Piccadilly train station in Manchester

d) Times Square subway station in New York City

ANSWERS

10) d	5) d
9) a	4) d
8) b	3) a
7) b	2) d
6) c	1) b

26

'All my crew are always saying I should act more diva-ish but there is not really much point. As long as I have my peppermint tea and salt and vinegar Snack-a-jacks, I'm all good.'

Going live

As the summer ended, Jessie's foot still hadn't healed properly, and she was forced to pull out of supporting Katy Perry on the US leg of her *California Dreams* tour. Jessie tweeted: 'Having a cry about having to pull out of the Katy Perry tour. I am as upset as my #heartbeats, believe me. My foot is just not healing as well as I hoped.'

She did have her own tour to think about, too. While Jessie had done a short seven-date tour around the UK back in April 2011, her *Heartbeat* tour would be her first ever major international one, beginning in October and November 2011 in England, Scotland and Wales, then continuing in spring and summer 2012 with dates in Australia, Singapore, Los Angeles, the UK and Spain.

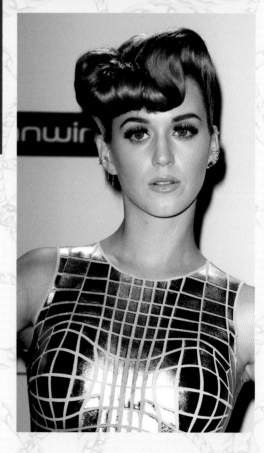

The Heartbeat Tour Setlist

1. Big White Room
2. Who's Laughing Now
3. Rainbow
4. Stand Up/One Love
5. Casualty Of Love
6. Nobody's Perfect
7. Never Too Much
8. Abracadabra
9. Technology/Up
10. L.O.V.E
11. Who You Are
12. Mamma Knows Best

ENCORE:
1. Do It Like A Dude
2. Price Tag
3. Domino

Winning

2011 was turning out – broken foot notwithstanding – to be a great year for Jessie. Her album was a hit, her tour was in full swing, and she was winning awards for her songs, album and style. In August, she was named Capital FM's Best Role Model In Pop, beating Lady Gaga, JLS, Justin Bieber and Beyoncé. 'Her songs tell you how life actually is and teach you what to expect out of it,' wrote one supporter on the radio website, while another commented, 'She likes life in the way she wants to and doesn't let anyone stand in her way'.

Jessie also won *Glamour* magazine's Woman Of Tomorrow award, *Harper's Bazaar* magazine's Breakthrough Of The Year award, music magazine *Q*'s award for Best Video (for 'Do It Like A Dude') and the Best Female Artist at the Urban Music Awards. But most impressive of all was the recognition she received at the MOBO Awards held in Glasgow on 5th October. Jessie won Best Newcomer, Best Album, Best Song (for 'Do It Like A Dude') and Best UK Act.

But that wasn't even the biggest event of the year for Jessie. For the day before the MOBOs she had made an announcement that would turn her from a critically acclaimed, successful pop/R&B singer into one of the biggest stars on British TV…

Just Jessie

'Some people might hate me, some people might love me.'

The Voice

In the summer of 2011 the BBC announced it would be making a new TV talent competition called *The Voice*. Based on a series that had originally started in Holland in 2010, *The Voice* in the USA had become one of the biggest shows of the spring, and it was expected to be just as successful in the UK.

In the US version, famous singers Christina Aguilera, Cee Lo Green, Maroon 5's Adam Levine and country music star Blake Shelton had been the judges, so the British version was expected to have big stars, too. On 4th October 2011 the first UK judge was announced... and it was Jessie J!

Becoming a mentor

The announcement was made on BBC Radio 1, and Jessie said: 'I can't wait, I'm so excited about it. I'm excited to be a coach, inspiration and mentor and I jumped at the opportunity as it's all about "the voice".' Danny Cohen, controller of BBC1 added: 'Jessie J is going to be an amazing coach on *The Voice*. She's a massive young star with a strong personality, and her recent MOBO nominations are testament to her musical and creative ability.'

Over the next few weeks Jessie's fellow judges were revealed – singing legend Tom Jones, rap star/producer will.i.am, and The Script's Danny O'Donoghue, while Holly Willoughby and Reggie Yates were confirmed as show's presenters.

The format of the show

So what was *The Voice* all about? The BBC described it as this: 'Four of the biggest names in music are looking for incredible singing talent to compete for the title of *The Voice* UK. Only the most unique and distinctive voices will make it to the filmed auditions and get to sing for our celebrity coaches.' Auditions began at the end of October, with wannabe singers from around the country performing for the show's producers. Once they had whittled the huge number of performers down to the best ones, it was time for the part of the show that made *The Voice* different from any other talent show that had gone before – the Blind Auditions.

The Blind Auditions

This, of course, is when the performers got to sing without the judges/coaches being able to see them! Jessie, Tom, Danny and will.i.am got to sit in high back chairs facing away from the singer so they had no idea what they looked like and could only judge them on their voice. If the judges were impressed with a singer, they could hit a button making their chair rotate so they could see the singer. If a singer got through, they worked with the judge of their choice as their coach. This was followed by the cut-throat 'Battle Phase', in which each judge had to pit their performers against each other to decide who went through to the live shows, where the public would get to vote, too.

Just Jessie

'The Voice is a show where I think I fit. The idea of being a coach and an inspiration and a mentor rather than a judge is something I can relate to.'

The biggest show on TV

The show was an instant hit, often beating *Britain's Got Talent* (showing at the same time on rival channel ITV) in the ratings, and fans were even treated to an extra-special performance on the show – the four judges singing 'I Gotta Feeling' together on stage! The four looked to be great friends, and Jessie added that she would love to record songs with all of them. 'Your career is about moments and things that inspire you, and all three of them are amazing artists.

I'd be honoured to work with any of them. I'd love to collaborate with Tom [Jones] especially, and I think that will happen very soon.'

She is clearly a fan of the legendary Welsh singer, so was surprised when the veteran asked her for advice, instead of the other way around! 'It was really nice that he's been part of a completely different musical background but he's interested in knowing about the things that I have to do now as an artist. I'm stepping into something new but he's also stepping into something new and we're both coming from different places. All of us learning from each other.'

Just Jessie

'It's very nice, very humbling to be accepted by someone like Tom Jones and for him to go, "Jessie, how do you think I should sing this bit?"

Jessie's Fellow Judges

Tom Jones

Sir Thomas John Woodward OBE is one of Britain's best-loved and most successful singers of all time. Now 72 years old, Pontypridd-born Tom began his career playing gigs at local dance halls and working men's clubs in South Wales, before he got a recording contract in 1964 with Decca. His second single for the label, 'It's Not Unusual' went to number one all over the world, and since then Tom has had more than 30 top 40 hits in the UK including 'Delilah', 'What's New Pussycat', his version of Prince's 'Kiss', and 'Burning Down The House' with The Cardigans. Tom can boast numerous successful tours, albums, and even a TV show (This Is Tom Jones) to his name, and has performed for both a US President (Bill Clinton) and the Queen for her Diamond Jubilee. Not bad for the son of a coal miner from Wales.

FACT: *Tom was good friends with Elvis Presley, whom he met in 1965. The pair spent lots of time in Las Vegas together, and remained pals until Elvis died in 1977.*

Danny O'Donoghue

Irish singer Danny is probably the least well-known of *The Voice's* judging panel. Born in Dublin in 1980, he started his music career in a band called Mytown in 1999 with pal Mark Sheehan, and when the group wasn't a success the pair found themselves being asked to write songs and produce records for other artists in the US. In 2005, they formed a new band, The Script, with young drummer Glen Power and in 2008 released their first single, 'We Cry'. Since then, the band have sold over 3.5 million albums worldwide, supported U2 on tour, and become one of Ireland's biggest acts.

FACT: Will Young was supposed to be a judge on The Voice, *but Danny was brought in to replace him as the producers wanted someone 'more rock', according to Young.*

will.i.am

Rapper, songwriter, DJ, singer and producer William James Adams was born in Los Angeles in 1975, and began rapping when he was in high school around Los Angeles before being discovered by Eazy-E in 1992. By 1997, Will had formed the Black Eyed Peas, and in 2001 the band hired Fergie to be their lead singer. Since then, the band has become one of the biggest in the world, and will.i.am has also found time to work as a record producer for artists including Michael Jackson, Britney Spears, Rihanna, Cheryl Cole and Justin Timberlake. He's acted, too, voicing Moto Moto in Madagascar: Escape 2 Africa, and starring as John Wraith in X-Men Origins: Wolverine.

FACT: *will.i.am suffers from tinnitus (ringing in the ears), a common condition among musicians who have been exposed to very loud music for long periods of time.*

The Voice vs the X Factor

'I don't support the *X Factor* putting through people that are just going to be made a laughing stock. That is one of the reasons why I won't be a judge on that show. That is not how I think the industry should be.'

JESSIE J

'We are our entity. We look after ourselves. We've produced some of the best talent you've seen in the UK ever. There was a moment last night in filming when all four coaches stood and remained stood up for the rest of the performance. We were so blown away by the level of the talent. I'm excited to just be part of this. I feel this is a game-changer in the UK scene.'

DANNY O'DONOGHUE

'When I first came to London in '63 and tried to get a record contract, they said that I looked too macho. So they were looking at me before they were listening to me, that hasn't really changed, and I don't agree with it. That's why *The Voice* is very important because there's no preconceived image. There's a lot of people out there and a lot of different kinds of music that needs to be made.'

TOM JONES

'I won't be a judge on *X Factor*. But *The Voice* is different. You can't even compare the two. On one, you have people in the music industry, current and legends, coaching the next generation. The other format you have judges critiquing, giving their opinions on things when they really don't know.'

WILL.I.AM

★ *The Voice* ★

You will need:

2 chairs, preferably with high backs!

Some friends!

A hairbrush

Music

There will be another series of *The Voice* soon, but in the meantime, why not invite some friends round and have your own auditions!

★ Set up the chairs in a room, so there is enough space for someone to stand and sing with the backs of the chairs facing them. This is so the judges can't see who is singing!

★ Choose two of your friends to be the judges (you can swap over later so everyone gets a turn).

★ You and your other friends each choose a song to sing along to – maybe one of Jessie J's!

★ Take it in turns to sing (using a hairbrush as a microphone, of course) – maybe see if the judges can guess which one of you is singing.

★ The judges should now judge who is the best singer, before they get a chance to swap over roles and sing themselves!

Jessie J: Steal her style

With her raven black hair and athletic figure, Jessie J is instantly recognisable and super stylish. Known for her catsuits and quirky outfits, Jessie can also rock an evening dress or look great in casual jeans and a T-shirt. Check out some of her most stylish moments... and then read on for tips on how to style yourself just like Jessie!

Daytime

It's clear from her onstage and offstage outfits that Jessie likes to have fun. Even when she's wearing jeans, she manages to make her outfit unusual by adding bling accessories (her favourites are huge gold hoop earrings), a fun hat or a T-shirt with a cartoon character on it. And it's the one time you don't have to worry about heels – Jessie's often been seen out and about in great big clumpy black biker boots!

Onstage

When you're on stage, you need to be able to move around easily, and Jessie's often rocked the audience while wearing snug-fitting jumpsuits in wild prints, or playsuits and corsets paired with eye-catching patterned tights. Try teaming a simple black dress with some multi-coloured tights and heels, or a brightly coloured (but plain) dress with black pattered tights and funky shoes. Jessie once teamed a fuschia-pink dress with a black biker jacket, black tights with 'Hollywood' printed all over them... and leopard print ankle boots!

Red carpet

Jessie is 5ft 9in tall, so she looks fantastic in a maxi dress. She has worn maxis with funky prints – leopard print, striking fluorescent art deco graphic and even a black and grey maxi dress with skeletons on it! The secret is to go for unusual styles rather than floral ones so you look modern rather than old-fashioned. If you're under 5' 5", go for a midi-length or shorter dress in a bright print. And don't forget those killer heels.

Get Jessie's sleek hairstyle

While her black bob is her most recognised hairdo, Jessie doesn't always keep it the same. She's had a high, slicked-back pony tail look, parted her hair at the side and made it wavy, worn it bright purple, had red streaks put in it, coloured the tips and even gone for a full volume curly look, too. What's her secret to great-looking hair?

Get that fringe

Even if you haven't got a fringe or shoulder-length hair, you can still get Jessie's sleek look as it works on most hair lengths. Here's how:

1 Wash your hair with a gloss or high-shine shampoo if you have one. Rinse well. Now massage in a shine/gloss conditioner and leave for a minute.

2 Rinse out the conditioner. Once your hair is clean, rinse one final time with cool or cold water – this helps your hair really shine.

3 If you have a leave-in shine serum for your hair, smooth a pea-sized amount through your hair, not forgetting the ends.

4 Divide your hair into sections. Taking one small section at a time, starting from the bottom, blow-dry your hair using a large round brush so you curl your hair under, towards your neck. You may need a friend to do this for you as blow-drying your own hair can be tricky! TOP TIP: If your hair is very fine and doesn't hold styles very well, once you have dried a section, wrap it around a Velcro hair roller to hold the curl while your hair cools.

5 Leave your hair to cool for a few minutes. Now gently brush your shiny locks, using the large round brush to help it curl towards your chin. Gorgeous!

6 For extra Jessie-ness, you can always try a temporary spray-in colour or some coloured hair extensions to brighten up your style.

Jessie J wordsearch

Can you find all ten words in the grid? Words may be written forwards, backwards or diagonally.

Jessica Cornish

Do It Like a Dude

Price Tag

Jessie J

The Voice

Pop star

London

Who You Are

Nobody's Perfect

Black bob

D	T	C	E	F	R	E	P	S	Y	D	O	B	O	N
O	B	J	E	S	S	I	E	J	C	P	Y	A	J	D
I	R	U	T	L	V	R	I	A	M	O	J	E	T	Z
T	T	A	Z	S	T	Z	O	B	C	P	S	R	A	B
L	C	V	O	M	P	U	P	L	T	S	N	A	D	S
I	P	J	A	G	N	I	G	A	I	T	L	U	P	L
K	J	R	X	S	O	A	E	C	P	A	V	O	F	B
E	E	S	H	T	D	U	A	K	M	R	N	Y	S	G
A	S	I	Z	L	N	C	G	B	U	D	N	O	B	A
D	E	B	C	A	O	A	A	O	D	F	B	H	O	T
U	D	U	I	R	L	G	E	B	T	P	H	W	V	E
D	M	Q	N	H	E	D	O	S	E	H	M	S	M	C
E	S	I	A	T	J	P	T	Y	M	N	S	I	K	I
O	S	I	L	R	U	V	S	H	C	F	X	T	O	R
H	B	T	H	E	V	O	I	C	E	B	S	A	V	P

Answers on Page 62

Get Jessie J's make-up look

Because she has dark hair and eyebrows, Jessie can carry off some striking make-up styles. The rule usually is to accentuate either your lips or your eyes, but with smoky eye shadow and bright red lips, Jessie does both and it works! What's more, she does it all herself: 'If someone did my make-up and my hair, and dressed me and wrote my songs, I wouldn't feel like me.'

Here's how to get dramatic eyes and lips just like Jessie's!

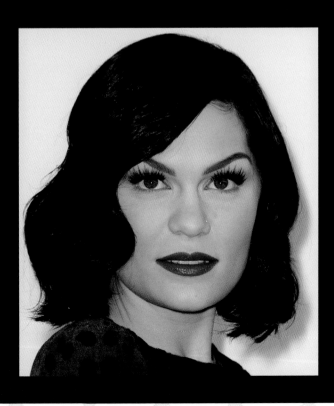

You will need:

Medium-coverage foundation

Concealer

Black or dark grey eyeshadow (go for the lighter option if you are blonde)

Silver or pale grey eyeshadow

Red or coral blusher (powder is easier than liquid)

Black eyeliner

Black mascara – and false eyelashes if you have some!

Eyebrow pencil, slightly darker than your eyebrows

Make-up brushes

Red lipliner pencil

Bright red lipstick (if you are very pale, you may want to use red lipgloss instead)

1 Before you start, make sure your face is thoroughly washed and cleansed and pat dry. Apply moisturiser to your face – not only is it good for the skin, it will also help your make up last longer.

2 Lightly dab foundation on your cheeks, forehead, nose and chin and blend it in gently with your fingertips or a foundation brush. Be careful not to use too much as you will get a dry, 'caked' look.

3 If you have dark circles under your eyes (tut, tut!), any blemishes or uneven skin tone, lightly touch liquid concealer to the trouble spots and blend in. If you need to, pop a little foundation over the top to even out the colour.

4 Suck in your cheeks so you can see your cheekbones. You want to apply blusher just above them. Place your blusher brush in the blusher and then lightly tap or blow off the excess powder. Brush upwards from the apples of your cheeks (above your cheekbones) towards your hairline at the sides of your face. Only use a tiny bit of blusher – it should just highlight above your cheekbones, not be two big red blobs of colour!

5 Using a small eyeshadow brush, apply the darkest shade (black/dark grey) on your eyelids, from the inner corner to the outside edge. Now take a slightly larger brush (or use your finger) and blend the shadow so it is softer and also flicks outwards and upwards at the outer corner of your eye.

6 Apply black eyeliner to your eyelids. You'll find a liquid liner is easiest – just follow the upper lash line from the inner corner of your eye to the outer edge and end with a little flick upwards at the outer corner of your eye. To get a steady line, rest your elbow on a table in front of a mirror and you'll find it easier and less messy. Also apply eyeliner to the lower lash line of your eyes – make sure you don't go inside your eyes with the liner as it will sting!

7 With the small brush or cotton wool bud, apply the paler (silver or grey) eyeshadow to the inner corners of your eyelids to brighten your look up. You can use the shadow to correct and hide any wobbles you may have had with the black eyeliner, too!

8 Now sweep mascara over your upper and lower lashes, starting at the base and working to the ends of your lashes. Don't 'pump' the brush into the mascara – all this does is push air in, which makes the mascara go clumpy quicker!

9 Brush your eyebrows (you can use a toothbrush if you don't have a brow brush!) to make them tidy. Very gently shade in your brows with the eyebrow pencil to darken them slightly and give them shape.

10 Outline your lips with the red lip liner. Using a tissue, soften the line a little, and then 'colour in' your lips with a bright red lipstick. Blot this lipstick well and then apply another layer. If you are pale and red lipstick looks too heavy on you, don't line your lips, simply apply a tinted red lip gloss to your lips.

You're now ready for your close-up!

Stylist for a day!

She's known for her amazing figure and her sense of style, and for being the one woman in pop who can really rock a catsuit. But could you dress Jessie better than she dresses herself? Here's your chance to style a star using the mannequins over the next few pages...

You will need:

Coloured pens

Glue

Scissors

Glitter or glitter glue

Sheets of coloured paper (or white a to colour on)

Using coloured paper, cut out clothes shapes using the outlines on the next few pages. (If you've got some tracing or greaseproof paper around the house, you can copy the outlines, trace them onto coloured paper and then cut the shapes out.)

Colour in and decorate the clothes any way you wish! You can add glitter, sparkles, flowery designs – whatever you like. Using the glue, stick your new outfit to the different Jessie J mannequins and she's ready to go out and have fun!

Daytime Jessie

On a cold English day, Jessie still manages to look cool in jeans and a blazer, often with a fun cartoon T-shirt, or patterned leggings. Don't forget to add some funky jewellery too – Jessie loves big hoop earrings and chunky necklaces, including her silver 'Jessie J' one that she has worn a lot.

Red carpet Jessie

When it comes to award ceremonies and red carpet moments, Jessie knows how to steal the limelight, often in stunning see-through gowns (with matching visible underwear, of course) and fitted maxi-dresses, as well as her trademark catsuits. Whether black or brightly coloured, her evening outfits are always striking, so go wild designing her a dress to be noticed in… and don't forget, she often matches her hair to her outfit (including wearing a purple wig) so remember to go crazy with her hair, too!

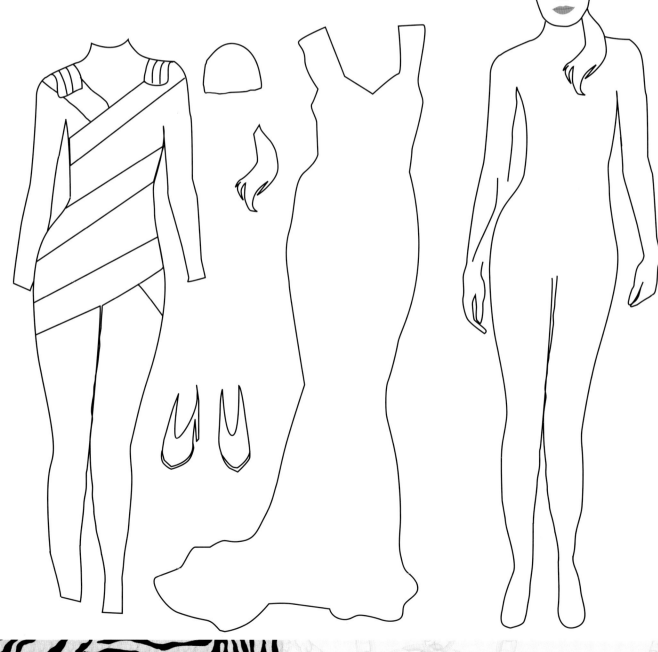

Pop star Jessie

Whether on stage or in one of her music videos, Jessie always wears memorable outfits, like a Union Jack bodysuit, fishnet dress, or fluorescent leotard. She even managed to make wearing a leg plastercast look cool when she broke her ankle in 2011 and continued to perform on stage! Jessie knows you need to stand out on stage so everyone can see you, so pick lots of colours for her outfit to help her stand out from the crowd!

Getting personal

While some stars like to chat about their love lives or be photographed on the red carpet with their best friends and family, Jessie likes to keep her personal life to herself to protect her nearest and dearest. She has revealed, however, five of the most important pals in her life, just for you:

Tinie Tempah

There have been rumours that Jessie and rapper Tinie became good friends, especially after they performed together at the Teenage Cancer Trust gig in March 2011. She was also seen cheering him on at the V Festival in August that year, but there isn't any romance on the cards. 'At the moment, I am single, and I'm happy and learning about myself,' she says. 'Music is the love of my life right now.'

Justin Timberlake

Justin's an actor, a singer and a megastar – and one of the first people to tell the world about Jessie's talent, after working with her on songs back in 2010. In an interview, Justin called Jessie the best singer in the world right now: 'Justin sat me down and said "you have the most incredible voice I've ever heard,"' remembers Jessie. Justin had first seen Jessie's YouTube videos and encouraged her to work hard to become a big star – and she took his advice! The pair have since written nine new songs together (Jessie even wrote one for Justin's ex, Britney Spears, but it has never been performed).

Ellie Goulding

Fellow singer Ellie and Jessie have become close friends since they both became famous. 'I'm really close with Ellie,' says Jessie. 'She keeps me sane as she's one of the people who can understand what my life is like.' Meanwhile, Ellie has said of their friendship: 'Me and Jessie talk quite a lot. I like that Jessie is so down-to-earth, and I like that we can just go out and talk about things.' In fact, Ellie even presented the Critics' Choice Award to Jessie at the BRIT Awards in 2011 – an award Ellie had won the year before!

Fearne Cotton

Fearne and Jessie are such good friends, they share the same hairdresser! Jessie admits she teases her good pal a lot and they often hang out on the red carpet at places like the BRIT Awards together. Jessie's also performed a few times on Fearne's Radio 1 show, and the pair spend time together trading fashion tips, too.

Katy Perry

Jessie and pop megastar Katy Perry became friends when Jessie agreed to be the support act for Katy's California Dreams tour. They were planning lots of fun after-concert parties and girls' nights – until Jessie injured her foot and was unable to join the tour! At the time, she tweeted: 'Having a cry about having to pull out of the Katy Perry tour. I am as upset, #heartbeats believe me. My foot is just not healing as well as I hoped.' Katy and Jessie have kept in touch, with Katy telling her followers to see Jessie in concert because she 'sings so good live!'.

Have a Jessie J Sleepover!

Invite your friends to a Jessie J sleepover – and why not tie the theme into Jessie's great belief that you should 'Be True To Who You Are', so everyone gets to choose their favourite things to wear and do!

You could:

Wear your favourite pyjamas

Make a sleepover music playlist, featuring all your favourite songs (including lots of Jessie J, of course!)

Paint each other's nails in your favourite colours

Watch your favourite movie together (Jessie's is *Titanic*!)

Eat cupcakes with your favourite toppings... yum!

You will need:

250g (8oz) unsalted butter, softened (get it out of the fridge an hour before you need it)

250g (8oz) caster sugar

250g (8oz) self-raising flour

pinch of salt

4 medium eggs

4 tablespoons milk

24 paper cases

2 muffin tins

How to make Jessie J cupcakes!

1 Turn the oven on to 190°C or Gas Mark 5 – it may be a good idea to get an adult to help you.

2 Put the butter in a large bowl and beat it (or use an electric whisk) until soft and creamy.

3 Add the sugar, flour, salt, eggs and milk and whisk until it's smooth with no lumpy bits.

4 Using a spoon (or, if you have one, an ice cream scoop) divide the mixture between all the 24 paper cases that you have put in the muffin tins.

5 Place the muffin tins in the oven and bake for 15 minutes. Swap the tins around and bake for another few minutes so all the cakes are a lovely pale gold colour.

6 To check that the cakes are cooked, take one tin out of the oven and place a skewer or cocktail stick in the centre of one of the cakes. If it comes out clean with no uncooked mixture on it, the cakes are cooked!

7 Take the tins out of the oven and leave to cool for a few minutes. Then remove the cupcakes from the tins and leave to cool on a wire rack.

8 The cakes are tastiest if you eat them on the day they are made, but you can freeze them – once the cakes are cool, pop them in freezer bags and put in the freezer for up to a month (they take about an hour to defrost when you need them).

9 When the cakes are cooled from the oven (or defrosted from the freezer) it's time to ice them!

For your sleepover, why not prepare a few toppings and icings in bowls, and let your friends decorate their own cakes exactly the way they want them? Here's a recipe for basic buttercream icing which you can add different flavours to:

You will need:

220g butter, softened

1kg icing sugar

2 tsp vanilla extract

120ml milk

1 Put the butter, icing sugar and vanilla extract in a large mixing bowl and beat with an electric whisk for about 5 minutes until it's smooth.

2 If the mixture is a bit stiff, add a little of the milk and whisk again. Keep doing this until the mixture is solid but spreadable. It's now ready to be put on a cake, or you can:

3 Stir in food colouring to turn the icing any colour you like – be careful, you only need a few drops!

4 Or add a few drops of liquid food flavouring (health food shops and supermarkets sell them) – there's almond extract, coffee extract, lemon flavour, orange flavour or even rose water essence to choose from!

5 Mix in chocolate chips for a crunchier topping.

6 Mix in edible glitter (available from supermarkets and cake making shops) for sparkly cakes.

7 Make chocolate buttercream icing! Just melt 400g of dark chocolate (at least 70% cocoa) in a bowl in the microwave – the best way to do this is to break the chocolate up first and microwave it for about 20 seconds, then stir, and then pop it back in again for 10 seconds if it hasn't melted enough. Keep doing this until it's melted but be careful, you don't want it to burn. If you don't have a microwave, place the broken up chocolate in a glass bowl and place that in a pan of boiling water (get an adult to do this) and stir the chocolate until it is melted. Let the melted chocolate cool slightly and then mix it into your plain buttercream icing mixture using a whisk.

8 Once you've chosen what topping to put on your cake, scoop a teaspoon of it and place it on the cake, then spread evenly with a knife. And don't forget you can add dry toppings such as chocolate chips, sweets, sprinkles, chocolate buttons, Smarties or mini marshmallows, too!

True or false quiz

Think you know everything about Jessie J? Then test yourself in our True Or False quiz to find out just how much you know about the 'Price Tag' star!

1) Jessie's real name is Jessica Cornwall.

2) She performed on stage in Andrew Lloyd Webber's musical *Whistle Down The Wind*.

3) The name of Jessie's girl band was River Deep.

4) Jessie wrote the song 'Do it Like A Dude' hoping Katy Perry would record it.

5) To date, she has sold over 12 million records worldwide.

6) Her TV show, *The Voice*, is based on an American talent show.

7) Jessie was the first judge to sign up to *The Voice*, with will.i.am, Tom Jones and Danny O'Donoghue signing up later.

8) Before she was famous, Jessie J had a song featured on the *Easy A* movie soundtrack.

9) The teddy bear in Jessie J's 'Price Tag' is missing an eye and a leg.

10) It took Jessie six years to make the album 'Who You Are'.

11) The 'J' in Jessie J's name stands for 'Justice'.

12) In 2011, Jessie broke a bone in her left foot while rehearsing.

13) When Jessie was growing up, she wanted to be Sporty Spice.

14) Jessie used to be on the same music label as Mr Blobby.

15) Jessie's favourite TV show as a kid was *Home And Away*.

How many did you get right?

Score: 5 or less
You love Jessie but are still getting to know her. Well, you've come to the right place – once you've read this book from cover to cover you'll be able to impress all your friends with your Jessie J knowledge!

Score: 6 to 10
Very good! You know Jessie well, but don't quite remember every little fact about her yet. Check out the other features about Jessie in this book and you're sure to score even better next time!

Score: 11 to 15
Well done! You know almost as much about Jessie as she knows about herself! Celebrate by listening to her album, and reading more about her in this book, of course…

Answers

1) False, it's Jessica Cornish.
2) True.
3) False, it was Soul Deep.
4) False, she wrote it with Rihanna in mind.
5) True – well done, Jessie!
6) False. There is a US version, but the first version of the show was The Voice of Holland on Dutch TV.
7) True.
8) True. Jessie recorded the song 'Sexy Silk' under her real name, Jessica Cornish
9) False, it's missing an eye and an arm!
10) True! She started writing it in 2005, and finished it in January 2011.
11) False. Jessie has said the J stands for 'whatever you want it to.'
12) True. She fell over on stage while wearing high heels!
13) True. She wouldn't have minded being Posh Spice either but said she didn't think she was pretty enough.
14) True!
15) False, it was Neighbours.

Jessie J's horoscope!

Jessie was born on 27th March 1988, which makes her an Aries. Arians are known as natural leaders (not a bad trait to have if you want to be a solo singing star – or a mentor on *The Voice*) and are often adventurous, direct, fearless and maybe even a little bit bossy! Arians are often athletic and sporty (no wonder Jessie looks good in her catsuits) and will happily argue their own corner if they think they are right. They are enthusiastic, eager, hard-working and determined... sounds like Jessie!

Other famous Arians include:

Victoria Beckham

Graham Norton

Keira Knightley

Lady Gaga

Elton John

Ewan McGregor

The year ahead

The next year is going to be a special one for Arians like Jessie. There is much prosperity predicted, but it will also be a very busy time with lots of travel involved – sounds like Jessie's second album will be a smash and she'll have to follow it with a tour perhaps?

There will also be lots of happiness and a person already in an Arian's life will come to be very special, influencing both work and personal life. Could romance be in the air? And who would be the lucky person in Jessie's life? Arians get on well with those born under the following signs: Leo, Sagittarius, Gemini and Aquarius.

Finally, those born under the Aries star sign have lots of energy and are always looking for new things to do and new worlds to conquer. She's already a pop star and a TV star, so perhaps Jessie will try other things in the year ahead: movie star? Fashion designer? Only time will tell!

The future

With a successful first album, number one singles around the world, and a hit TV show behind her, there's no stopping Jessie J. After releasing her second album, Jessie has promised to embark on another tour, and she has also hinted that she would like to do many other things, too, including writing a stage musical for London's West End and Broadway, launching her own clothing line and her own perfume, too!

With a talent like hers, it's certain all her dreams will come true. Just watch this space…

"You have to take what life throws at you and do it well and do your best, and I can only give what I can give and try to do my best."

Jessie J

Credits and Acknowledgements

Getty Images
4, 5, 7, 10 (bottom), 12 (left), 13 (top), 14 (top), 15,16, 17, 19, 20, 22, 24, 27, 28, 30, 35, 36, 37 (left), 38, 40 (left), 41 (bottom), 42, 44 (top), 45, 46, 50, 51 (top), 55, 56, 60, 61

Rex Images
2, 6, 8, 9, 10, 11, 12 (right), 13 (bottom three), 14 (bottom), 18, 21, 23, 25, 26, 29, 31, 32, 33, 34, 37 (right), 39, 40 (middle, right), 41(top, middle), 44 (bottom), 51 (middle, bottom), 52, 53, 57, 58, 59

ACKNOWLEDGEMENTS
Posy Edwards would like to Jo Berry, Jane Sturrock, Nicola Crossley, Helen Ewing, Rich Carr and Smith & Gilmour

Copyright © Orion 2012

First published in hardback in Great Britain in 2012 by Orion Books an imprint of the Orion Publishing Group Ltd
Orion House, 5 Upper St Martin's Lane, London
WC2H 9EA

An Hachette UK Company

1 3 5 7 9 10 8 6 4 2

A CIP catalogue record for this book is available from the British Library.

ISBN: 978 1 4091 1005 7

Designed by Smith & Gilmour
Printed and bound in Germany bound by Mohn Media

The Orion Publishing Group's policy is to use papers that are natural, renewable and recyclable and made from wood grown in sustainable forests. The logging and manufacturing processes are expected to conform to the environmental regulations of the country of origin.

Every effort has been made to fulfil requirements with regard to reproducing copyright material. The author and publisher will be glad to rectify any omissions at the earliest opportunity.

www.orionbooks.co.uk

Jessie J wordsearch answers

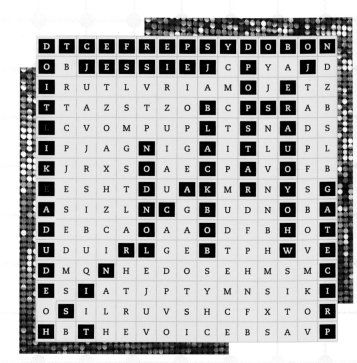